EXPLORE ANCIENT ROME!

CARMELLA VAN VLEET
ILLUSTRATED BY ALEX KIM

green press
INITIATIVE

Nomad Press is committed to preserving ancient forests and natural resources. We elected to print *Explore Ancient Rome!* on 50% post consumer recycled paper, processed chlorine free. As a result, for this printing, we have saved:

12 Trees (40' tall and 6-8" diameter)

4,921 Gallons of Wastewater

1,979 Kilowatt Hours of Electricity

542 Pounds of Solid Waste

1,066 Pounds of Greenhouse Gases

Nomad Press made this paper choice because our printer, Thomson-Shore, Inc., is a member of Green Press Initiative, a nonprofit program dedicated to supporting authors, publishers, and suppliers in their efforts to reduce their use of fiber obtained from endangered forests.

For more information, visit www.greenpressinitiative.org.

Questions regarding the ordering of this book should be addressed to

Independent Publishers Group

814 N. Franklin St.

Chicago, IL 60610

www.ipgbook.com

Nomad Press

2456 Christian St.

White River Junction, VT 05001

Contents

For Mom and Abbey—my bookends.

Other titles from Nomad Press

Let's Explore Rome!

Have you ever used a calendar or walked on a paved road? Have you ever been to a mall? Do you have running water in your house? If so, you can thank the people who lived in ancient Rome! Ancient Romans invented these things and many more.

Where was ancient Rome? What was the **Roman Empire**? What was it like to live there? And, how did ancient Rome influence the world we live in today?

In this book, you'll explore ancient Rome, an incredible city and empire that existed from 753 BCE to 476 CE. This book will also answer many of your questions and share some cool facts.

1

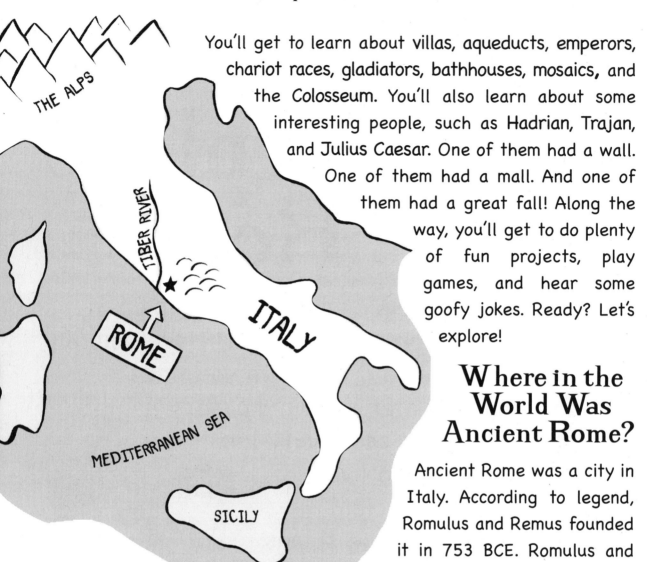

You'll get to learn about villas, aqueducts, emperors, chariot races, gladiators, bathhouses, mosaics, and the Colosseum. You'll also learn about some interesting people, such as Hadrian, Trajan, and Julius Caesar. One of them had a wall. One of them had a mall. And one of them had a great fall! Along the way, you'll get to do plenty of fun projects, play games, and hear some goofy jokes. Ready? Let's explore!

Where in the World Was Ancient Rome?

Ancient Rome was a city in Italy. According to legend, Romulus and Remus founded it in 753 BCE. Romulus and Remus were brothers who were taken from their mother and left to die along the banks of the Tiber River. A she-wolf took care of them until a shepherd adopted them. When they got older, they decided to build a city near the place the wolf found them. They fought over who would rule the new city and Romulus killed Remus. Rome, which still exists, is named for Romulus.

The area, which had seven hills, was a good place for a city. The Tiber River provided water, food, and a way to travel. In time, the rulers of Rome took over neighboring lands. All of these lands together were called the Roman Empire. The Roman Empire grew to include Spain, Greece, Asia Minor, Britain, Turkey and North Africa. The Roman Empire also controlled the Mediterranean Sea.

Because the Roman Empire was so big, different parts had different kinds of weather. Some places were cold. Others were hot. There were also different kinds of landscapes. Some places had desert sand. Other places had mountains. Romans became good at adapting to different kinds of environments. This helped them grow and flourish. One of the other things that helped ancient Romans to thrive was the **aqueduct.**

WORDS to KNOW

Roman Empire: all the lands and people ruled by Rome.

aqueduct: a channel that carried water from streams in the hills and mountains and from the Tiber River to the city of ancient Rome.

channel: a canal through which a stream of water moves.

castellum: a water tank in ancient Rome.

Cloaca Maxima: a famous sewer in Rome—the first sewer.

1000 BCE   750 BCE   500 BCE   250 BCE   0   250 CE   500 CE   750 CE   1000 CE   1250 CE   1500 CE   1750 CE   2007 CE

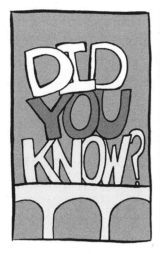   

Aqueducts

A million people lived in ancient Rome. All of those people needed water. In order to get water to the city, Romans built aqueducts. Aqueducts were **channels** that carried water from streams and springs in the hills and from the Tiber River to the city. They were made out of stones and concrete and had gradual slopes to move the water down. Gravity makes water move downhill.

At first, these channels were underground. This was probably done to hide the aqueducts from enemies. When the Roman Empire got so big it didn't have to worry about enemies as much, the aqueducts were built above ground, on top of concrete archways.

Cool Artifact

Ancient Romans discovered a way to make concrete waterproof. They added volcanic sand. This was important because it meant they could build things that lasted a long time and held up in all kinds of weather. An example of this is an aqueduct. Many ancient Roman aqueducts are still standing, even though they are no longer used.

Water moved through the aqueducts into the city. There, the water flowed into a water tank called a **castellum.** Next, water was sent into pipes that led to public bathhouses, fountains, and the homes of the wealthy. Poor people got their water from the fountains. Each day, the aqueducts carried over 200 million gallons of water into the city.

There were valves to turn off the water, but the Romans didn't use them unless there was a problem. This meant water ran 24 hours a day. You'd probably get in trouble if you left the water running all day long!

To help drain all the used and dirty water, Romans invented sewers. The first sewer was called the **Cloaca Maxima**. It was about 985 yards long. It was tall enough, in places, for a horse and cart to go through! This sewer is still used today, 2,500 years after its construction.

Roads

Along with aqueducts, roads played a very important role in ancient Rome's success. In order to allow quick travel to the city, ancient Romans built the first paved roadways. All of these roads led from various cities straight into Rome.

And straight was right! Ancient Romans built roads that took the shortest possible route. Sometimes, this meant building a road right through a hill. There were no curves.

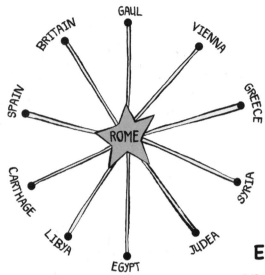

WOW

There is an expression that says, "All roads lead to Rome." It means that no matter which direction you go or decision you make, you'll end up in the center of things or at the same place. This saying comes from the fact that all the roads in the Roman Empire led to the city of Rome like spokes on a wheel.

Ancient Romans built their roads with great skill. First, they dug out a foundation. Then, they laid sand or gravel down. Finally, they carefully placed stone slabs or paving stones on top. Each roadway had a slightly raised center so that water would run into drainage ditches along the side. This kept the roads from getting muddy and slippery. The ancient Romans built their roads so well that many are still used today.

then & now

then: the beautiful archways that supported aqueducts decorated the land. Sometimes, houses were even built nearby so people could enjoy them.

now: the beautiful archways are still part of modern Rome's landscape. Tourists come from all over the world to see ancient Roman arches.

Make a Keystone Puzzle

How does an arch stay up? It's because of the keystone. A keystone is a specially shaped stone at the top of the arch that is the "key" to an arch.

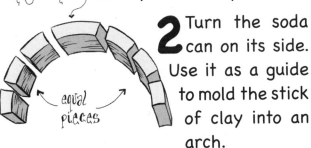

keystone?

equal pieces

1 Lay a piece of wax paper on your workspace.

2 Turn the soda can on its side. Use it as a guide to mold the stick of clay into an arch.

3 After your arch is formed, slide the can out from underneath it.

4 Lay the arch down on the wax paper. Use the knife to cut a "keystone" out of the top of the arch.

5 Next, cut the rest of the arch into six, equal pieces. When you're done, you should have one keystone and six supporting pieces (three for each side of the arch).

6 Let the clay pieces harden. Make sure they aren't touching as they dry.

7 Once the clay pieces are hard, see if you can put them together to build an arch. You can use the soda can to support your arch until you add the keystone. If you'd like, you can also ask a friend to help you hold the pieces.

How hard is it to put your keystone puzzle together? How important is the keystone? Let a friend or family member try to put the puzzle together.

Supplies

wax paper

soda can, either opened and empty or closed and full

1 stick of air-hardening clay, any color

knife (if you use a sharp knife, be sure to ask an adult for help)

Make an

You will be using pointed scissors for this project, so ask an adult to help.

1 Turn the shoebox over so the open part is facing down. At the end of one of the long sides of the box, make a mark 1½ inches from the bottom.

2 Use the ruler to make a straight line from this mark to the bottom corner of the opposite end of the box. You're making a triangle. Cut along the line. Do the same thing on the other long side of the box.

3 Cut the extra piece of cardboard off the short end of the box. When you're done, your box should slope.

4 Use the pointed tip of your scissors to poke a hole near the top of the plastic bottle. Cut the top off. Poke a hole near the bottom of the bottle and cut the bottom off. You should now have a cylinder.

5 Cut the plastic bottle in half, lengthwise. Put the two pieces of bottle together so that they form a long channel. Overlap them slightly and connect them with duct tape.

6 Fold several pieces of duct tape with the sticky sides out, and use them to attach the channel to the shoebox. It's okay if the plastic channel hangs off the ends of the box.

Supplies

shoebox (without the lid)
ruler
pencil or pen
pointed scissors
1-liter plastic bottle
duct tape
shallow bowl
cup of water

Aqueduct

7 Place your bowl at the low end of your aqueduct. Slowly pour the water into the high end. The water should run down the channel into the bowl. Think of some fun ways to use your aqueduct. Maybe you could use it to water a plant or even to pour milk into your cereal bowl!

Make a

Ancient Romans used simple tools to build their roads, homes, buildings, and aqueducts. One of these simple tools was a plumb bob. A plumb bob uses gravity to help a make a straight line. Plumb bobs worked so well that many carpenters and builders still use them today!

1 Spread the newspaper over your workstation. Next, mix a small amount of plaster of Paris according to the directions on the container.

2 Pour the plaster of Paris into one of the egg cups, filling it to the top.

3 Place the paper clip into the plaster of Paris so that the top third of the paper clip stays above the plaster surface. Slide the toothpick through the paperclip, then let the toothpick rest across the top of the egg cup to keep the paperclip in place. Let the plaster of Paris dry completely.

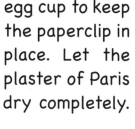

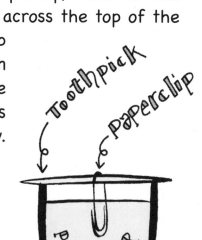

Supplies

newspaper
plaster of Paris
water
small bowl
styrofoam egg carton
large paperclip
toothpick
1 yard of heavy string
scissors

Plumb Bob

4 Next, remove the hard plaster from the egg cup. (You might have to peel the carton off.) This will be the weight for your plumb bob.

5 Tie one end of the string to the paperclip. Now your plumb bob is ready to use!

Have a friend hold the string about 3 inches from the wall. Allow the weight to swing freely. Wait until the weight stops swinging. Just let gravity do its work! When the weight is still, you will have a straight line from the top of the string to the bottom of the string. You can use that to guide you as you mark a straight line on the wall with a pencil.

Roam Like a Roman

Ancient Romans built their roads completely straight whenever possible. They did this because they wanted to travel quickly from one place to another. Start from any room in your home and pretend your bedroom is the capital city, Rome. You need to get there taking the shortest route. Walking only in straight lines, see how many steps it takes to get to your room. If you have to, you can change the direction you're walking but no walking in a curve! How many steps does it take to go from the kitchen to your room? How about from the living room? How much faster do you think it would be if there were no walls in your house?

Home Sweet Villa

Most ancient Romans worked in the city. But not all of them lived there. The wealthy lived in beautiful, country homes called villas.

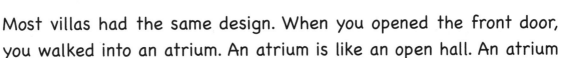

Most villas had the same design. When you opened the front door, you walked into an atrium. An atrium is like an open hall. An atrium usually had an opening in the ceiling to let in light and small pools in the floor for decoration. The other rooms were around the atrium. A villa had a dining room, an office/reception area, and bedrooms. A kitchen and bathroom was at the back of the house.

The rich could even afford flushing systems for their toilets! Villa walls were covered in beautiful **mosaics** and **frescoes**. Mosaics were pictures made from hundreds of tiny tiles or stones set in cement. Frescoes were a kind of wall painting in which paint was applied to wet plaster.

Ancient Romans loved gardens. And most villas had one. Villa gardens were usually round or rectangular. They were filled with plants, trees, flowers, statues, and marble fountains. They often had decorative fish pools. Sometimes, they housed fancy birds, like peacocks.

Slaves took care of the gardens. A slave is a person who, in the eyes of the law, belongs to another person. It seems strange to us, but having slaves was normal in ancient Rome.

City Living

For those who were poor, housing was terrible. The poor often lived in the city in cramped, block-style apartments called **insulae**.

14

These apartment buildings were above shops and could be three to six stories high with hundreds of rooms. The smallest rooms were on the top floor. This is where the poorest people lived.

These buildings weren't made well and sometimes fell down. And, because they were made with wooden framework, these dwellings caught fire often. To keep the risk of fire down, kitchens weren't allowed. People bought prepared food from food carts.

Many of the apartments probably had bathrooms. These bathrooms did not have a flushing system, though. People used chamber pots and emptied them into the sewers or cesspits. Other times, people just used public bathrooms.

WORDS to KNOW

mosaic: a picture made from hundreds of tiny tiles or stones set in cement.

fresco: a kind of wall painting in which paint is applied to wet plaster.

slave: a person who, in the eyes of the law, belongs to another person.

insulae: a block of apartments in ancient Rome.

Ancient Roman Bathrooms

Ancient Romans had public bathrooms. The bathrooms had long, stone benches with numerous openings. Some of these benches could hold a dozen or more people. There were no stalls. People just sat down and visited with the other people nearby. Instead of toilet paper, ancient Romans cleaned themselves with wet sponges tied to sticks. Waste was flushed away with water into the city's sewer system.

WORDS to KNOW

bathhouse: public, indoor pools where Romans met to relax and socialize.

strigil: a long, metal tool ancient Romans used to scrape dirt off their bodies.

paterfamilias: the male head of a household.

Ancient Romans (rich or poor) had the same kinds of furniture. Most people had three- or four-legged tables, couches for eating and sleeping, oil lamps, and cupboards or chests. The rich had armchairs whereas the poor used benches. Both had strong boxes to lock away valuables.

Bathhouses

Public **bathhouses** were very popular in ancient Rome. They were large buildings with enough indoor pools for hundreds of people. Nearly everyone, rich and poor, visited the the public bathhouse several times a week. It cost very little to go. Romans didn't swim in the pools, though. They went there to get clean, visit with friends, exercise in the bathhouse yard, and even read. Bathhouses were the number-one hangout spot!

then & now

then: ancient Romans had bathhouses. Tourists can still see some of the ancient bathhouses.

now: there are community centers or gyms where people socialize and exercise.

16

Bathhouses had several rooms, ranging from cold to hot. First, bathers undressed and left their clothes in a locker room area. Next, there were three main areas they could visit. One had pools with cold water. This area was called the *frigidarium*. The next area was known as the *tepidarium*. This had pools with warm water. The last area was the *caldarium*. This had heated pools.

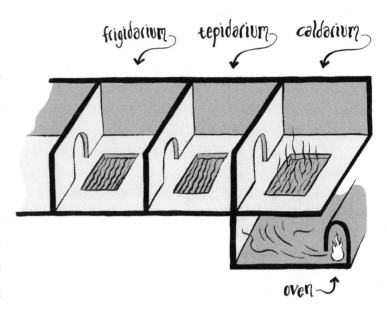

frigidarium tepidarium caldarium

oven

Slaves kept fires burning to heat a space underneath the pool floors. The heated air warmed the water. Sometimes, the pool floors in the bathhouses were very hot. Bathers wore wooden shoes to protect their feet.

JUST FOR LAUGHS

Q: What did the ancient Roman do when he got into the pool and realized he'd forgotten his pool shoes?

A: He hotfooted it out of there!

Ancient Romans didn't use soap. They rubbed olive oil on their skin and scraped off dirt with a long, metal tool called a **strigil**. Men and women did not bathe together. They used separate bathhouses or went to the bathhouse at different times of the day. Children did not go to bathhouses.

The Lost City

The Roman Empire had lots of towns and cities. One of the most famous cities is Pompeii. Why is Pompeii famous? Because it was buried!

Pompeii was a beautiful, bustling city at the bottom of Mount Vesuvius. Mount Vesuvius is a volcano near Naples, Italy. In 79 CE, it erupted. People tried to get away, of course, but the poisonous gases from the volcano killed them in their homes or on the streets. Soon, everyone and everything in Pompeii was covered in at least 10 feet of volcanic ash. Thousands of people died, and the city was abandoned and forgotten. But some good came out of the tragedy. You see, when the ash settled on top of the city, everything was preserved. The ash protected buildings, beautiful artwork, and everyday items. By studying these things, we have learned a lot about how the ancient Romans lived. Another interesting thing the ash did was make casts of the dead people and animals. The actual bodies are long gone, of course. The casts are kind of creepy but, at the same time, very interesting. We can still see the casts, along with the rest of Pompeii, today. The lost city was discovered in 1748 and later restored.

Cool Artifact

The English word *family* comes from the Latin word *familia*. In ancient Rome, a family included everyone and everything in a household. The father was completely in charge. He was called the **paterfamilias**.

Make a Mosaic

Many ancient Roman homes had a mosaic by the front door. It was a picture of a dog and the words: *Cave Canem*. This is Latin for "Beware of Dog." The sign was supposed to scare off burglars. Here is an easy way to make a painting that looks like a mosaic made with round stones.

1 Spread the newspaper over your work area. Lay the foam board on top.

2 Use the pencil to lightly sketch a picture on your foam board. Some mosaics were of people. Some were landscapes or objects. Others had patterned designs. If you'd like, you could even draw a dog for your own "Beware of Dog" sign.

3 When you're happy with your picture, you can begin painting. Dip the end of a Q-tip in the paint. Press the Q-tip on the foam board to make a dot. Use dots to go over the outline.

4 Once you have the outline done, use more dots to fill in the rest of the picture and the background. Keep the dots close to each other. Be patient. It might take a long time to make that many dots!

5 When the paint is dry, you can hang your mosaic in your bedroom and imagine you're back in ancient Rome.

Supplies

newspaper
black foam board cut to any size you want
pencil
2 dozen Q-tips
acrylic paint in various colors

Make an

Ancient Roman gardens often had decorative columns. On these columns, Romans hung sun catchers called oscilla. They were made of terracotta or white marble and had pictures of gods on them.

1 Cut a circle (or disc) out of your cardboard. You can cut several if you want to make more sun catchers. An easy way to make a circle is to place a drinking glass or round cookie cutter onto your cardboard and trace around it.

2 Use the pointed tip of your scissors to carefully poke a hole near the top of your disc. Ask a grown-up to help with this. Tie a long piece of string or ribbon onto your disc.

3 Place your disc on a flat surface covered with newspaper. Use the fabric paint to draw a picture or a design on one side of the disc. Be sure to keep your design simple. If you make it too detailed, the paint will run together.

Supplies

cardboard
scissors
string or ribbon
newspaper
paint brush
fabric paint, any color
white craft paint

Oscillum

4 Carefully pick up the disc by holding on to the edges. Flip it over and paint a design on the other side. Ask a friend or grown-up to hold the disc for you while you paint. Don't worry, the fabric paint on the other side shouldn't drip. But be sure not to bump it against your body or clothes.

5 Use the string or ribbon to hang up the disc. Let the paint dry completely. This may take a day or two.

6 After the paint is dry, spread newspapers on your work area and use the white paint to paint both sides of the disc. Let the paint dry. Now, your oscillum is ready. Just hang it near a sunny window and enjoy!

Make a Bottled

Ancient Romans enjoyed sitting in their gardens. It made them feel at peace. In this project, you can make your own indoor garden to admire. You will need to ask an adult to help you.

1 Ask an adult to help you cut the top third of the bottle off. Don't throw this away; you'll need it later.

2 Pour the stones into the bottom of the bottle. The stones will help with drainage. Put a half-inch layer of activated charcoal on top of the stones. The charcoal keeps the soil and plants from rotting.

3 Cut the screen into a circle with a diameter of 3½ inches. Lay the screen on top of the charcoal. The screen helps keep the soil from settling into the charcoal and stones. Put about 3 inches of soil on top of the screen.

Garden

4 Plant your plants in the soil. Put the tall ones in the back. You can add small, decorative rocks, shells, or aquarium decorations to make your garden more interesting. After you're done arranging your plants, water them until the soil is moist.

5 Tape the top third of the bottle back on. (You can also just slide the top part over the bottom part.) Leave the cap on.

6 Place your bottled garden in a sunny area. After a few days, you might notice beads of water on the inside of the bottle. Don't worry; this is supposed to happen. If your garden seems too wet, take the cap off for a day. Water as necessary to keep your garden moist.

Supplies

scissors

clear, 2-liter plastic bottle with cap

small stones such as aquarium rocks

activated charcoal found with aquarium supplies

small piece of screen

potting soil

3 small plants, such as African violets or cacti

decorative rocks, shells, or aquarium decorations (optional)

water

clear tape

Make a Strigil

Strigils were metal tools ancient Romans used to scrape dirt off their skin at the bathhouse. You'll be using wire cutters for this project, so ask an adult to help.

1 Unwind and straighten the wire hanger. This can be a bit tricky, and you might need to ask a grown-up for help. Use the wire cutters to cut the hanger so that you have a piece of wire 18 inches long.

2 Wrap a few small pieces of masking tape around both ends of the wire. This will help prevent the ends from poking out later on and hurting someone.

3 Cut a piece of cardboard that is half an inch wide and 4 inches long. Tape this piece of cardboard along the last 4 inches of wire on one end.

4 Bend your wire into the shape of a strigil. A strigil looked kind of like an opened letter "J" without the top. They could also look like an "S" that's been stretched out.

5 Once you have the shape you want, cover the wire and the cardboard with aluminum foil. Squeeze the foil tightly so it stays in place.

6 Tape several small cardboard pieces around the end opposite your 4-inch cardboard piece to make a handle. You can also cover this end with aluminum foil.

Supplies

**wire clothes hanger
wire cutters
masking tape
small piece of cardboard
aluminum foil**

Eat Like a Roman

ARoman family's diet was based largely on how much money they had. Poor people ate a lot of simple breads and soups, and vegetables such as onions, peas, celery, and lentils.

Every once in a while they ate fish or meat. They also ate a lot of stew that was basically just water and grain mixed together. The government gave free grain to those who couldn't afford it.

The rich had a diet with more variety. It included lots of the same vegetables, but also fresh fruits, pastries, and eggs, as well as meat from pigs, chickens, and geese. One popular dish had dormice in it. A dormouse was a kind of rodent that looked like a tiny squirrel. This might sound strange to us, but the Romans thought it was delicious!

Roman farmers kept livestock such as oxen, geese, and chickens. They grew vegetables such as onions, garlic, celery, lettuce, and peas, and fruits like figs, apples, and pears. (Grain came mainly from Egypt.) The most important crops, though, were grapes and olives. The Romans used grapes to make wine. Olive oil was used in cooking, to fuel lamps, to clean the body, and to keep the skin soft. Both wine and olive oil were stored and shipped in special pottery jars called **amphorae**.

Romans ate little during the day. The morning and midday meals were light. But the evening meal, which was eaten in the late afternoon, was usually the main meal of the day. Although they had knives and spoons, these utensils were only used for serving. Romans ate with their fingers.

Strange But True

Romans used many spices. Thyme, parsley, oregano, ginger, coriander, mustard, rosemary, and pepper were all popular. They put pepper on everything, even dessert! Romans didn't have sugar—instead they sweetened things with honey.

The most popular seasoning, though, was garum. Garum was a sauce made with fish intestines, salt, and other flavorings. It had a very strong taste. It smelled terrible while it was being made, because the ingredients were left out to **ferment** for several weeks. The smell was so bad that people weren't allowed to make garum in or near the city. Luckily, once it was done, garum didn't smell bad.

Romans usually ate their everyday meals at tables. But when they threw a dinner party, wealthy Romans lay on couches to eat! The custom was to lean on the left arm and eat with the right hand. Formal dining rooms had low tables that were surrounded on three sides by couches, called triclinium. Three adults could lie on a couch to eat. Kids usually ate sitting on stools near their parents. The fourth side of the table was kept open so that servants could bring plates of food. Dinner parties could be very fancy affairs with lots of food and with entertainment such as storytelling, music, and dancing.

WORDS to KNOW

amphorae: pottery jars used to store wine and olive oil.

ferment: the process where something with a lot of energy, such as grain, breaks down into a simpler substance, like beer. Wine, yogurt, and vinegar are all products of fermentation.

Cool Artifact

Ancient Romans ate a kind of pizza called ofellae. This was bread topped with onions, fish, and olives. There were no tomatoes or cheese toppings. Later on, those foods came from other countries.

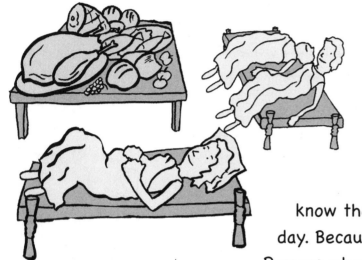

Feasts could last for hours. When guests got full, they left the party and made themselves throw up so they would have room for more food!

You might be surprised to know that a lot of Romans ate out every day. Because of the danger of fires, poorer Romans who lived in city apartments were not allowed to have kitchens. They bought their food from street vendors or at inexpensive restaurants called *thermopolia*—the ancient Roman version of fast-food restaurants!

then & now

then: ancient Romans had a very light breakfast. Many times they had only a bit of bread and water.

now: people in Rome still eat very small breakfasts. A typical breakfast is a sweet roll and coffee.

Trajan's Market

Trajan was a great Roman emperor. Under his rule, the Roman Empire grew to its largest size. To celebrate his victory over the Dacians, a people who had resisted Roman rule for many years, Trajan built a great marketplace. It was known as **Trajan's Market** and was built in the shape of an arc into the side of a hill. You could say Trajan's Market was the first indoor shopping mall! It was two stories high and had 150 shops and offices. These shops sold everything: oil, wine, seafood, vegetables, fruit, and other groceries. Trajan's friend Apollodorus of Damascus designed the market. Workers started building it in 107 CE and finished in 110 CE. Though the shops have long been empty, you can still visit Trajan's Market in modern Rome.

Near the market is **Trajan's Column**. This is a 100-foot-high marble column decorated with pictures that tell the story of Trajan conquering the Dacians. The pictures are carved into a horizontal panel, called a **frieze**, that wraps in a spiral around the whole column. The story in pictures begins at the bottom of the column and ends at the top. It was designed so that people could "read" about Trajan's great victory.

JUST FOR LAUGHS

Q: What did one knife say to the other knife right before the big Roman dinner party?

A: Look sharp!

29

The Roman Forum

There were a number of large open areas called **forums** throughout the city of ancient Rome. A forum was paved with stone, decorated with beautiful fountains and statues, and surrounded by buildings and shops. People gathered at the forums to visit, do business, or shop. Rome's central and most famous forum, called the Roman Forum, was surrounded by many important temples, where Roman gods were worshiped, and **basilica**, where government business was conducted.

WORDS to KNOW

Trajan's Market: a two-story, indoor market with 150 shops. It was built during the reign of the emperor Trajan.

Trajan's Column: a 100-foot-high column carved with scenes of Trajan's victory over the Dacians.

frieze: a narrow horizontal, decorative panel.

forum: an open area, or town square, where Romans shopped or met to do business.

basilica: the public building used as a courthouse or gathering hall.

Make a Delicious Dormice Dish

This cooking activity uses a stove. Ask an adult to help. Be sure to wash your hands before you begin.

1 Follow the directions on the cereal box to make Rice Krispies Treats. Ask an adult to help you since you'll need to use the stove.

2 Let the mixture cool for a few minutes. Take a licorice string and wrap a small handful of the cereal mixture around one end. The licorice will be your mouse's tail.

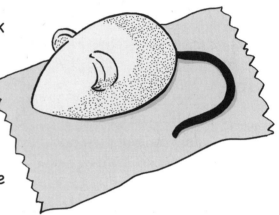

3 Shape the cereal to look like a mouse's body. Roll the mouse in the chocolate cookie crumbs. The crumbs will be your mouse's fur. Place the mouse on wax paper.

4 Use the remaining mixture and licorice to make more mice. When you're done rolling all the mice in cookie crumbs, use the frosting to make two beady eyes on each mouse.

5 Now, you're ready to put your dormice on a plate and serve your friends a tasty version of an ancient Roman treat!

Supplies

**Rice Krispies cereal
margarine or butter
bag of marshmallows
large saucepan
wooden spoon
black licorice strings
chocolate cookie crumbs
wax paper
red gel frosting**

Make an Amphora

1 Cut the top quarter off one of the bottles. You can recycle the rest of this bottle and the lids. You won't need them.

2 Tape the top of the first bottle to the top of the second bottle. The openings should be facing each other.

3 Roll several pieces of newspaper into a log. Cut the newspaper log in half. Use the pieces to make two C-shaped handles.

4 Tape the handles, one on each side, to the open end of the bottle.

5 Cover your work area with plenty of newspaper. Mix 2 cups of flour with 1 cup of water in your bowl to make papier-mâché.

6 Tear the rest of the newspaper into strips. Dip the strips into the flour and water mixture. Wipe off any extra paste and place the strips over the bottle and the handles.

Supplies

two plastic bottles
(one- or two-liter bottles work)
scissors
masking tape
newspaper
flour
water
small mixing bowl
string (optional)
red or brown craft paint
and brush

7 Cover the entire bottle, inside as much as possible and outside, as well as both handles with strips of newspaper. You can use a bit of string to hang your bottle from a chair or doorframe while you work so that you can cover the bottom, too. Put several layers of papier-mâché on your bottle.

8 Let the bottle dry completely. Once your amphorae is dry, you can paint and decorate it.

Make a Round Loaf of Bread

You'll need a grown-up to help with this cooking project.

1 In the bowl, mix 1 cup of flour with the yeast and salt. Stir in the warm water, and mix well. Add the remaining flour and stir until blended.

Supplies

large bowl
wooden spoon
3 cups all-purpose flour
1 package active dry yeast
¾ tsp salt
1 cup warm water
clean kitchen towel
greased baking sheet
oven preheated to 375 degrees
sharp knife
aluminum foil
honey

2 Sprinkle a little flour on your work area. Take the dough out of the bowl and put it on the floured surface. Knead the dough until it is stiff and elastic. This will take about 10 minutes.

3 Clean the bowl and grease it, then shape the dough into a ball. Place it back in the bowl and cover the bowl with the towel. Put the bowl in a warm place. Let the dough rise until it doubles in size, about an hour.

4 Take the dough out of the bowl and punch it down. Roll it gently on the floured surface. Let the dough rest for about 10 minutes. While you wait, you can grease the baking sheet.

5 Shape the dough into a round loaf and place it onto the greased baking sheet. Cover the dough with the kitchen towel again.

6 Put the dough back in a warm place and let it rise until it doubles in size again. This will take about an hour. Preheat the oven after about 45 minutes.

7 Once the dough has risen, have your adult helper use the sharp knife to make some criss-cross cuts on the top of the loaf. The cuts should be about a quarter-inch deep.

8 Ask an adult to put the bread dough in the oven. Bake the loaf for 20 minutes.

9 After 20 minutes, cover the loaf with a sheet of aluminum foil. This will keep the loaf's crust from getting too brown. Bake for 15 minutes more. Remove the loaf from the oven and let it cool. Slice or tear off pieces, dip them in honey, and enjoy!

Make Your Own Frieze

Trajan's Column has a frieze that shows him defeating the Dacians. You can make a column that shows you doing or achieving something special!

1 Cut the paper into four strips that are 2 inches wide and 11 inches long. Tape three of the strips together. Save the fourth strip in case you need it.

2 Use the markers to tell a story with pictures. Draw about a time you did something special: when you went on vacation, learned to ride a bike, got a pet, made a snowman, or won an award. Or, you could make a timeline of your life. Start when you were a baby and draw the important events in your life.

3 When you are finished drawing, tape the beginning of the frieze near the bottom of the Pringles can or mailing tube. Tape the paper strip at an angle.

Supplies

piece of white, 8½-by-11-inch paper
ruler
scissors
Scotch tape
markers
empty Pringles can or mailing tube

4 Wrap the frieze around the can, taping it to the can as you go. You can use the extra strip of paper to fill in the space at the top and at the bottom of the can. Decorate this extra space with a pattern.

5 Now, share your column with a friend, grandparent, parent, or a brother or sister. See if he or she can read your picture story!

Variation: If you use a can with a lid, ask an adult to cut a slit in the lid. Put the lid on the can and your frieze column can double as a piggybank!

Host a Roman Dinner Party

Hosting a Roman dinner party is easy! All you have to do is spread out a small tablecloth on the floor—with a grown-up's permission, of course! Place some couch cushions or pillows around the tablecloth. Put on some music. Invite your guests to lie down and eat with their fingers. What to serve? Try some of these ancient Roman foods: grape juice (instead of wine), olives, grapes, figs, pears, hardboiled eggs, salad, celery sticks, and rolls. You can also serve honey with your own round loaf of bread.

Time for School

Today, almost all children have the chance to get an education, whether they go to public school, private school, or are home schooled. In ancient Rome, only the children of wealthy families had a formal education.

In poorer families, boys learned a trade from their fathers, and girls learned how to take care of the household and younger children from their mothers. Kids who went to school attended primary school from about age 7 to age 14. **Primary school** classes were usually held in a public place, such as forum.

A primary school teacher, called a pedagogue, taught children how to read and do math. Most of the learning was done by rote. This means children had to memorize information.

then & now

then: Romans used letters to represent numerals.

now: Roman numerals can still be seen on many things, such as on watches and in the Super Bowl title!

Addition and subtraction were done on an **abacus**. An abacus was an early calculator. People could keep track of numbers by moving beads or counters along a rod.

Most children did not go beyond primary school, but a few continued to **grammar school**, where they learned Greek and Latin grammar. Grammar school students were taught at home, usually by Greek teachers. (The Greeks were known for being well-educated.) Even fewer students continued beyond grammar school to the highest level of education, **rhetoric school**.

In rhetoric school, a teacher called a rhetor taught children the art of public speaking. Being a public speaker was a very important job. Because many ancient Romans couldn't read, public speakers announced city business and other important news and information. These public speakers were called **orators**.

WORDS to KNOW

primary school: a public school where Roman children learned reading and math.

abacus: an early calculator using beads on rods to add and substract.

grammar school: a school where Roman children learned Greek and Latin grammar.

rhetoric school: a school where Roman students learned to be good public speakers.

orators: public speakers.

Knucklebones: a Roman game where players tossed small bones into the air and tried to catch them on the backs of their hands.

Toys and Music

When they weren't doing chores or learning, Roman children liked to play and have fun. Many of their toys were similar to the toys you probably have. They had dolls, marbles, balls, and board games such as checkers. These toys were not made of plastic or rubber, though. Kids used other things to make toys. For example, children made dolls out of rags. They made dice, which was a popular game in ancient Rome, out of bones or stones. And, instead of having portable or permanent game boards, they drew boards right on the ground!

One very popular game in ancient Rome was **Knucklebones**. To play Knucklebones, players tossed small bones into the air and tried to catch them on the backs of their hands. The bones came from the anklebones of a sheep.

Music was a popular pastime in ancient Rome. Children and adults enjoyed listening to musicians play in the streets. Street musicians played many kinds of instruments: pipes, flutes, cymbals, tambourines, lyres (a kind of small harp), rattles, horns, and castanets. Professional musicians played at dinner parties.

Cool Artifact

Roman children didn't do schoolwork on paper. They wrote on wax tablets. Children used a pointy tool called a stylus to etch letters and numbers into the wax. To erase work, children just smoothed the wax with their hands.

Roman Numerals

Ancient Romans used letters to show numbers. Have you ever seen a clock or watch with Roman numerals? Sometimes, at the end of a movie, you'll see Roman numerals. Here are the basic numbers:

I = 1   L = 50   M = 1,000
V = 5   C = 100
X = 10   D = 500

All the other numbers are made by combining letters. For example, if you want to show the number 9, you would write IX. This is a kind of shortcut to show you mean the number that is "one less than ten." If you want to show a bigger number, you add on to a letter. For example, the number 12 is written as XII (10 + 1 + 1 = 12). How old are you? See if you can figure out how to write your age in Roman numerals.

Latin

Ancient Rome's official language was Latin. The word "Latin" came from *Latium*, the name of the area where Rome was built. Latin is the basis of many modern languages: Italian, French, Spanish, and Romanian. Unlike our alphabet, early Latin had 23 letters. The letters "I" and "J" were considered the same letter as were the letters "U" and "V". There was no letter "W." Here's something else that's interesting about Latin. It was originally written in all capitals. There were no lowercase letters!

Lots of words we use in the English language are derived from Latin. Here are just a few of them: actor, author, census, college, congress, item, library, novel, pupil, senate, ultra, and veto.

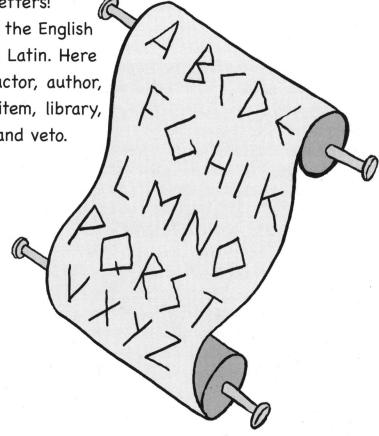

JUST FOR LAUGHS

Roman version:

Q: Why was IX afraid of VII?

A: Because VII "VIII" IX!

English version:

Q: Why was 9 afraid of 7?

A: Because 7 "8" 9!

Make Your Own Marbles

1 In your bowl, mix the sawdust, flour, and just enough water to make dough. The dough should be kind of stiff but still easy enough to squeeze. If the dough gets too soupy, add more flour and sawdust. Knead the dough until it stretches like bread dough.

2 Take the dough out of the bowl and put it on the wax paper. Pull small pieces off and roll them into marble-sized balls. Make 20 small balls and 2 slightly larger balls. These larger balls will be your shooter marbles.

3 Let the marbles dry in the sun for several days. They should be very hard.

4 Paint half of the marbles one color and the other half the other color. After the paint dries, you're ready to play!

* Ask a hardware store or lumberyard for sawdust. Have an adult carefully take out any pieces of wood or large splinters.

To play marbles:

Draw a circle with a piece of chalk in the dirt. You can also use a piece of long string to make a circle. Each player should place his or her smaller marbles somewhere inside the circle. Using the shooter marbles, each player takes turns trying to hit the other player's marbles out of the circle. The first person to knock out all of his or her opponent's marbles, wins.

Supplies

bowl
2 cups fine sawdust*
1 cup all-purpose flour
water
wax paper
acrylic paint, two different colors
string or chalk

Make Your Own

Some ancient Roman children went to special schools to learn how to speak well in public. Pubic speakers, called orators, were in charge of reading any important government business to the Roman people. These announcements were usually written on pieces of paper rolled up into a scroll. These scrolls had handles so orators could unroll them easily.

1 Roll up several pages of newspaper, width-wise, to make a paper log. Make sure the roll is tight.

2 Wrap masking tape around the entire newspaper log. Put a few pieces of tape over the ends, too. This will be one of your scroll handles. Make a second handle just like the first one.

3 Tape the three pieces of paper together lengthwise. You should have one piece of paper almost a yard long when you're done.

4 Write anything you want on the paper: a school or family announcement, a poem, a story, the lyrics to a song, the top 10 places you'd like to visit, or a birthday wish list.

Supplies

newspaper
masking tape
3 pieces of 8½-by-11-inch paper, any color
pen, pencil, or markers
string or ribbon (optional)

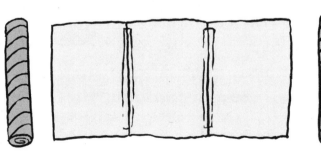

Scroll

5 Tape one end of the long piece of paper to the back of one of the handles. Tape the other end of the long piece of paper to the back of the other handle.

6 Roll up the scroll by rolling each handle toward the middle of the paper. You can keep the scroll together by tying a piece of string or ribbon around it.

7 When you're ready to read your scroll, stand up. Roman orators usually stood to read. Next, hold the bottom handle still and gently pull the top handle up to unroll the scroll.

Be Glad You're Not a Gladiator!

What do you like to do for fun? Ancient Romans had many different forms of entertainment. Some of the things they enjoyed were the same kinds of things we enjoy today.

Other forms of their entertainment, though, were things that might seem very strange or cruel to us.

Theater

Everyone in ancient Rome liked going to the theater. The theater was exciting and it was free! Ancient Romans borrowed many of their plays from the Greeks. Their favorite kinds of plays were tragedies and comedies. A **tragedy** is a sad play. A **comedy** is a funny play.

Roman actors were admired. They were kind of like today's television and movie stars. They were also almost always men. Actors wore costumes and brightly painted masks. These masks showed whether a character was male or female. They showed how a character was feeling, too. For example, actors wore a smiling mask if the character was supposed to be happy.

The biggest theater stars were the people who performed **pantomime**. A pantomime is a play that tells a story through body movement or facial expressions. It doesn't use words. In ancient Rome, dancers mimed (acted out) the action while a narrator told the story. Often, music was added to the performance.

WORDS to KNOW

tragedy: a sad play.

comedy: a funny play.

pantomime: a story told through body movement or facial expressions, without any words.

JUST FOR LAUGHS

Q: What did one Roman actor say to the other?

A: Can you play?

47

The first theaters in Rome were made of wood that was torn down after the play was over. Later on, the Romans built many large and beautiful theaters made of stone. These theaters had no roofs; they were open to the sky. The stage was at one end of the theater. The audience sat in front of the stage. The rows of seats were in **tiers**, similar to the seats we find in stadiums or auditoriums today. Theaters were different sizes. Some could hold 9,000 people. Others could hold as many as 80,000 people!

A Day at the Races

Like the theater, **chariot** races were free. And, boy, did ancient Romans love to watch chariot races! A day at the races was even more popular than a day at the theater.

Chariots are small vehicles with wheels and a platform. Chariots were pulled by two, three, or four horses. Riders stood on the platform and controlled the horses as they raced around the track for seven laps. Chariot racing was very dangerous. This is because horses are large and quick animals. Also, chariot racing had few rules. These two things meant there were lots of crashes. Riders had to carry a special knife—called a falx—to cut themselves from a wreck. It didn't always help. In fact, many chariot racers died.

Circus Maximus

Romans built large racetracks for chariot races. One of the biggest was built by the Roman emperor Trajan and was called the **Circus Maximus**, meaning "great circle." It was oval-shaped, over 1,960 feet long, and about 650 feet wide. The Circus Maximus could hold over 250,000 spectators at a time. On a full racing day, spectators saw up to 24 races. Today, not much is left of the Circus Maximus. But visitors can still see the open area where the dirt track once was.

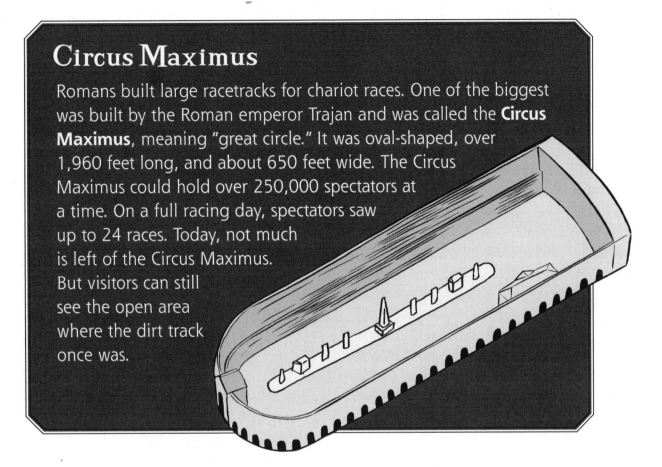

Riders raced for teams. There were four teams: Red, White, Blue, and Green. Each team had loyal fans. Sometimes fans got out of control and fought with each other. Racers did anything they could to win, even if it meant cheating. For example, some racers would ram their chariots into other racers' horses! They wanted to win so badly because the prize money, called a purse, was very large. A purse could be up to 60,000 sestertii, the coins used by ancient Romans. In a whole year a Roman soldier earned only about 1,000 sestertii. So, this was a lot of money! But the money wasn't the only reason riders loved to win. Chariot racers were very famous. They were like our sports stars.

The Colosseum

The **Colosseum** was the greatest **amphitheater** in the entire Roman Empire. Made of stone and concrete, it used a beautiful system of arches, stairways, and hallways to lead to seating. Each section of seats was marked with numbers. It was very much like sports stadiums today! The Colosseum could hold over 50,000 people. But what all those people went to watch is something we'd find gruesome.

What went on inside the Colosseum was the bloody sport of **gladiator** fighting. Gladiators were men who were forced to fight to their deaths while audiences watched and cheered. Most of them were slaves or criminals. A few of them were people who needed money so badly that they volunteered to fight. Sometimes, gladiators were trained at a special school. But most of the time, they had little training. They were simply led into the arena and left to fight. If a slave or criminal fought well enough, he might be able to win his freedom. Most gladiators died after only a few fights.

Gladiators fought other gladiators. Some were heavily armed. For example, they might be given a sword or a three-pronged weapon called a **trident**.

The Colosseum is one of the world's most famous buildings.

50

Other gladiators only had fishing nets or daggers. Others had no weapons at all. Many times, an unarmed gladiator would have to fight a heavily armed gladiator. Before each match, the two gladiators faced the emperor (who sat in a special seat) and said, "Those who are about to die salute you!" Then, the bloody battle would begin.

then & now

then: ancient Romans liked to watch gladiators battle each other to the death.

now: soccer, called football outside the United States, is Italy's favorite sport.

The men would fight until one person was killed or quit. When someone decided to quit, he would signal by raising his index finger. The emperor would then decide his fate. If the emperor thought the gladiator had fought well, he would give a hand signal that showed the gladiator would be allowed to live.

If the emperor felt the gladiator had fought poorly, he would give another signal. Then . . . it was the end of the road. The gladiator was killed and dragged off. Many Hollywood movies show emperors giving the "thumbs up" or "thumbs down" sign. We don't know for certain if these were the hand signals real ancient Roman emperors used.

Cool Artifact

Some gladiators wore armor. Armor included shields, protective coverings for arms and legs, and helmets. Some helmets covered the gladiator's whole head, with only two small holes for his eyes!

Gladiators also fought animals. Romans brought all kinds of exotic animals to Rome from around the world: bears (even polar bears!), rhinos, lions, tigers, and elephants. Animals were often starved or treated cruelly. This caused them to be more likely to attack or kill a gladiator. Often, gladiators didn't see the animals coming because they would be released from hidden cages or brought to the arena through trap doors.

Even though we find gladiator fighting very cruel and strange, the ancient Romans loved it. This was just the way things were back then.

WORDS to KNOW

tiers: rows arranged one above another.

chariot: small vehicle with wheels and a platform, pulled by horses.

Circus Maximus: an ancient Roman chariot racetrack.

Colosseum: the biggest and most famous amphitheater in Rome.

amphitheater: an oval or circular building with rising tiers of seats around a central open space. Used in ancient Rome for spectacles and contests.

gladiators: slaves and criminals who were forced to fight for sport.

trident: a kind of pitchfork.

Interesting Colosseum Facts

🌿 The ancient Romans called the Colosseum the Flavian Amphitheater. This is because Flavius was the family name of Emperor Vespasian, the emperor who started construction of the Colosseum in 70 CE, and Titus, the emperor who finished it in 80 CE.

🌿 The Colosseum is 164 feet tall, 617 feet long, and 512 feet wide. It's so big that five professional football fields could fit inside!

🌿 The Colosseum has 80 entrances.

🌿 Animal fights took place in the Colosseum. Thousands of animals died each day.

🌿 The arena's floor was covered in sand. The Romans used sand because it helped absorb blood.

🌿 The Colosseum had a canvas roof that could be put up or taken down.

🌿 The arena floor could be flooded so mock sea battles could take place.

🌿 The Colosseum had elevators that used a counterweight system. These elevators helped bring animals up to the arena floor.

🌿 Lightning and earthquakes damaged the Colosseum, but some of it still stands today.

Make a Roman Theater Mask

Supplies

newspaper

plastic one-gallon milk jug, rinsed and dried

pointed scissors

plastic wrap

large roll of plaster cloth, sometimes called plaster gauze*

shallow bowl of water

decorating materials such as paint, yarn, glue, and markers

heavy string (optional)

* You can find this with the plaster of Paris in many craft, hobby, or art supply stores. Rigid Wrap is one brand name.

Roman theater masks had exaggerated features. This means a smiling mouth or frowning eyebrows were really big! You'll be using pointed scissors to cut a plastic jug for this project. Ask a grown-up to help.

1 Cover your workspace with newspaper. Cut off the bottom of your milk jug so you have a "bowl" about 2 inches high. Turn the bowl over and place it on the newspaper. This will be the mask's base. Cover the base with a sheet of plastic wrap.

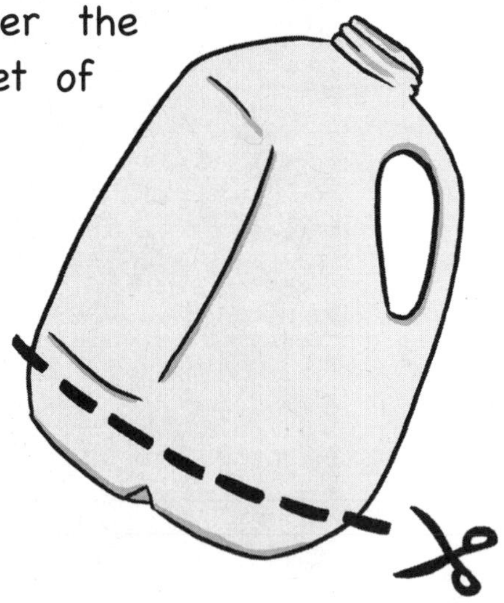

2 Cut the plaster cloth into triangles. This shape will lie flat better than square pieces. Dip the pieces in the water and lay them on the base. You can make your mask into any character or emotion by shaping the pieces of cloth. Be sure to leave two eyeholes so you can see out of your mask.

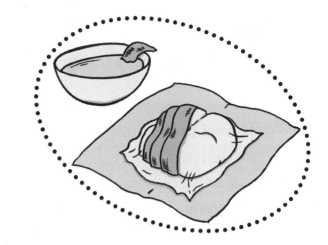

3 Let the mask dry completely. Carefully lift it off the base and peel away the plastic wrap. Trim any extra cloth from around the edges of the mask.

4 Decorate your theater mask using paint or markers. You can add some hair using yarn and glue. When your mask is done, hold it up to your face and pretend you're a Roman actor! If you want to tie the mask onto your head, use heavy string. Use the pointed scissors to poke holes in the sides of the mask. Thread the string through the holes and tie knots to secure it.

Play Charades

Pantomiming was very popular in ancient Rome. Charades is a game where players take turns pantomiming actions or activities, titles of movies or books, and phrases or sayings while other players try to guess them.

1 Divide into two teams. Each team should write a variety of actions on the notecards—one action on each card. (For a more challenging game, write some book or movie titles and phrases, too.) Here are a few ideas to get you started: swimming, shooting a basketball, running, reading, planting a garden, eating, getting dressed, skateboarding, kicking a ball, answering the phone, sleeping.

2 Put the notecards face down in a pile. Have one person choose a card from the other team's pile. That player pantomimes the action for his or her own teammates. The team tries to guess what is being acted out.

3 Then it's the other team's turn. One person picks a card from the first team's pile and mimes the action. Keep playing until everyone has had a turn.

Variation: Try to tell a whole story by acting it out. Don't use any words. See if your audience can figure out which story you're performing. Here are some good stories to try: *Goldilocks and the Three Bears*, *Jack and the Beanstalk*, or the *Three Little Pigs*. Of course, you can also make up your very own story!

Supplies

**a group of friends
notecards
pencil
space to move around**

High Fashion

The Roman Empire was very large. It included many lands and all the people of these lands wore different styles of clothing. In Egypt, for example, the people wore simple tunics and see-through dresses.

The Celtic people wore long, woolen shawls, and trousers. But what did the people who lived in the capital city of Rome wear?

Ancient Romans must have liked comfortable clothes. We can guess this because the most popular piece of clothing was the **tunic**. A tunic was a simple, loose-fitting garment. It looked kind of like a long, sleeveless T-shirt. Men's tunics were knee-length. Women's tunics were ankle-length. Tunics were usually white and made of linen. Rich and poor people wore tunics. But if you were rich, you wore other layers of clothing. Rich Roman women wore a long dress called a **stola** over their tunics. They also wore a shawl called a **palla**. Rich men wore **togas** over their tunics. A toga was a long, dress-like wrap. Wealthy men and boys were expected to wear togas in public. Once at home, though, they probably took them off. Togas were made of wool, so they were hot and uncomfortable to wear!

Colors

Colors were an important part of Roman fashion. Common or poor people dressed mainly in white clothes. This is because dyes could be expensive. The rich liked to wear bright colors. Women from wealthy and powerful families wore clothing dyed with shades of red, yellow, orange, and blue. Dressmakers made colored cloth using plant dyes. Roots of the madder plant were used for red. Leaves of an herb called woad were used for blue. The crocus plant made yellow.

A man from a wealthy and powerful family, such as a **senator**, would wear a toga with a purple edge. A young boy from a wealthy family would wear a thin band of purple on the edge of his toga. Once a boy turned 16 and was considered an adult, he wore a wider band of purple on his toga. The emperor wore a purple toga with a gold band on the edge. Purple dye was made from shellfish. It was very difficult and expensive to make, so that's why it was a symbol of wealth.

Hair and Makeup

Roman women loved wearing makeup and having styled hair. They often had slaves whose only jobs were to apply makeup and style hair.

In ancient Rome, pale skin was considered fashionable because it showed that a woman didn't need to spend time working in the sun. Before putting on red or pink rouge and green or blue eye shadow, Roman women applied white powder foundation to their skin. This powder was made from lead. It was poisonous, and some people believe it probably made women sick! Rouge and eye shadow were made from other minerals and plants.

Slave women wore their hair short, but free Roman women grew their hair long. For most of ancient Roman history, women's hairstyles were simple. They usually just pulled their hair back into ponytails or buns.

Later on, rich women began wearing curls. These curls were made with a hollow, heated rod of iron called a *calamistrum*. It was the first curling iron! Curls were kept in place with ribbons and hairpins made of bone and wood. Wigs were also popular. Many wigs were made with the blond hair of German women. Most ancient Roman women had dark hair. Blond hair was different and therefore considered special and very fashionable.

Ancient Roman men usually had short hair. For most of Roman history, they didn't have beards or mustaches. Keeping their faces hairless was a tough thing, though. There were no razors or scissors, so barbers removed facial hair with tweezers. Ouch! But when Emperor Hadrian grew a beard to hide a scar on his chin, beards became the fashion. Kind of like how famous people start fashion trends today!

Jewelry

Both men and women wore rings. They were usually made of gold, silver, or bronze. Women also wore bracelets, earrings, and necklaces. Men and women kept their clothes in place with a pin called a **fibula**. This was the Roman version of a safety pin. They also used brooches, decorative pins with a clasp, to keep clothes in place. Both men and women sometimes wore cameos. Cameos were small carvings, usually of a person's profile.

then & now

then: Romans wore mainly tunics, togas, and stolas made of wool or linen. Pants weren't considered fashionable.

now: people who live in modern Rome wear lots of different clothes, including pants and jeans.

60

A profile is the side view of someone's face. Cameos were often carved out of coral and worn as rings or brooches.

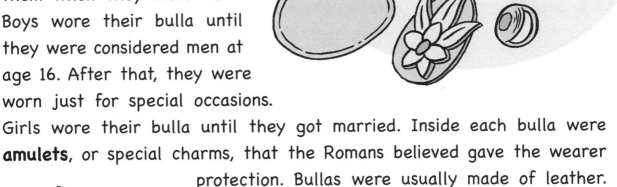

All children wore a special locket-like necklace, called a **bulla**, that was given to them when they were born. Boys wore their bulla until they were considered men at age 16. After that, they were worn just for special occasions. Girls wore their bulla until they got married. Inside each bulla were **amulets**, or special charms, that the Romans believed gave the wearer protection. Bullas were usually made of leather. But rich children had bullas made of gold, silver, or bronze.

WORDS to KNOW

tunic: a simple, ancient Roman garment that looked like a long, sleeveless T-shirt. Both men and women wore tunics.

stola: a long dress worn by ancient Roman women.

palla: a rectangular, woolen shawl worn by women.

toga: a long, dress-like wrap worn by men.

senator: a government official in ancient Rome.

fibula: a special pin used by both men and women to hold their clothes in place.

bulla: a locket-like necklace given to each child at birth. There were amulets inside the bulla.

amulet: special charm that protects the wearer.

Make a Tunic

If you use a sewing machine for this project, you'll need a grown-up's help.

1 First, you have to figure out how much material you'll need. Use the tape measure to measure from your shoulders to your knees (if you're a boy) or to your ankles (if you're a girl). Next, multiply that length by two.

2 Lay your material flat. Measure and cut your material to the length you need. Then fold it in half. Cut about 5 inches from one of the long sides. Save this strip of material. You can use it to make a sash. Don't cut the fold or you'll cut the sash in half.

Supplies

2 to 3 yards of light-weight material, such as an old sheet

tape measure

scissors

fabric glue OR a sewing machine

fabric paint, beads, or other things to decorate your tunic

3 Cut a "T" shape out of your material. Then cut a small, half oval from the middle of the top, folded edge. This will be your neck hole.

4 Use the fabric glue to seal the sides of the body and the underside of each sleeve. You could use a sewing machine to sew a one-inch seam in these areas instead.

5 Turn the tunic inside out so the glue or seams don't show.

6 Most Romans wore simple, white tunics. But, you can use the fabric paint and beads or sequins to decorate yours if you'd like. You can also use strips of material you cut in step 2 as a sash or belt.

7 When the fabric paint has dried, slip into the tunic and slip into history!

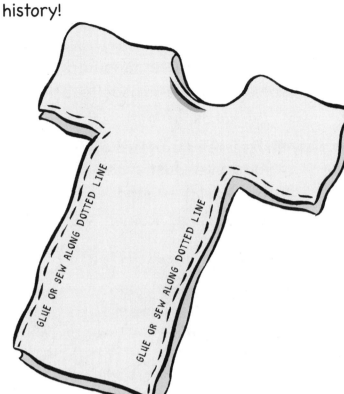

GLUE OR SEW ALONG DOTTED LINE

GLUE OR SEW ALONG DOTTED LINE

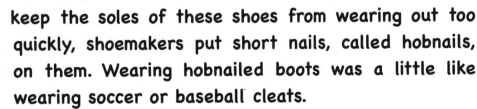

WOW Ancient Romans wore a variety of shoes. The most common type was a loose-fitting, leather sandal that looked kind of like a slipper. Poor people and farmers just wore strips of animal hide wrapped around their feet. Soldiers—who did a lot of walking—wore leather sandals or a leather boot with laces. To keep the soles of these shoes from wearing out too quickly, shoemakers put short nails, called hobnails, on them. Wearing hobnailed boots was a little like wearing soccer or baseball cleats.

Make a Palla

A palla was a rectangular, woolen shawl that women in ancient Rome wore. They were usually brightly colored. To make one, all you need is 1½ yards of material. You can choose any color you'd like. Pallas were made of heavy material but you can use a lightweight material if you'd like. Just make sure the material you use drapes easily. Wrap the material around your shoulders like a shawl. To look more like a real ancient Roman woman, wear your tunic underneath. Let the extra material drape over your arms. Now, you're stepping out in high, Roman fashion!

JUST FOR LAUGHS

Q: What did the toga maker say when he was done making the toga?

A: That's a wrap!

Make a Toga

1. Lay your material on the floor. Open it up if you haven't already.

2. Cut the material into a half circle that is 4 feet long and about 4½ feet wide. The size of your half circle should depend on how tall you are. If you are tall, make it bigger. If you are short, make it smaller.

3. If you want a purple edge, now is the time to paint it on your toga. Let the paint dry before moving on. Remember: boys under the age of 16 had a thin, purple band around the edges of their togas.

To put your toga on:

Here is the easiest way to put your toga on: Use a safety pin to secure one end of the material near your waist. (You can wear your regular clothes or your tunic underneath.) Wrap the material around your waist at least once, then throw it over your left shoulder. Pull the material toward your waist and use a safety pin to keep it in place. You'll probably need a friend or grown-up to help you with this part. You can rearrange the material to get it just the way you like.

Supplies

3 to 4 yards of white muslin*

scissors

purple fabric paint OR a purple marker (optional)

safety pins

* An old sheet that's been cut in half won't work quite as well, but it will do in a pinch. Plus, it's a great way to recycle an old sheet!

Make a Bulla

You will be using spray paint and a hot glue gun for this project, so ask a grown-up to help.

1 Cut a piece of string long enough to fit over your head. Tie the two ends together.

2 Spread out newspaper to cover a large work area. Read the instructions on the can of spray-paint. Spray-paint the outside of the mint tin and the string. Let the paint dry.

3 Once the paint is dry, open the tin and spray-paint the unpainted areas. Turn the string over and paint the other side, too.

4 When the paint is dry, use the hot glue gun to attach the string to the back of the tin. The string should be near the edge of the tin, wherever you want the top of the bulla to be.

5 Decorate the outside of the bulla with sequins or markers, if you'd like.

6 Now you can put an amulet—a good luck charm—inside your bulla. Some ideas: a lucky penny or pebble, a rabbit's foot, or a lucky rubber band.

Supplies

heavy string
scissors
newspaper
brown, bronze, or gold spray-paint
1 small breath mint tin (not plastic), rectangular or circular, with a top
hot glue gun
sequins or permanent markers (optional)
good luck charm

Emperors Rule!

Throughout its history, ancient Rome was ruled in three ways. First, Rome was ruled by a handful of **kings**. We don't know the exact number, but it was around seven.

Beginning about 509 BCE, groups of people worked together to rule Rome. This period of time is known as the **republic**. And finally, **emperors** ruled Rome.

This time period is called the **empire**. It is these last two types of government that Rome is famous for.

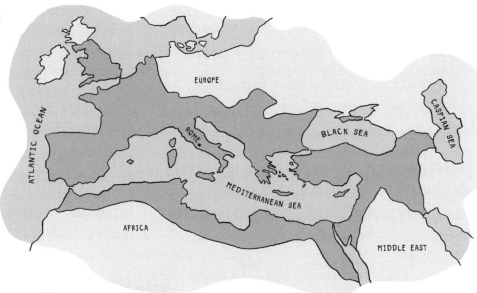

☐ ROMAN LANDS DURING THE EMPIRE

The Republic

Kings ruled Rome starting in 753 BCE. After the last Roman king was overthrown in 509 BCE, Rome became a republic. A republic is a government system of elected leaders. During this time, a group called the **Senate** governed Rome. There were about 300 members of the Senate, and they were called senators. Senators were men who usually came from families who had lived in Rome a long time and who had lots of money. This was good since senators weren't allowed to have another job! It was the senators' responsibility to decide on big things, such as laws and which lands should become part of the Roman Republic. Every year, senators also elected two **consuls**. Consuls were government officials who took care of military business.

There were other groups within the Senate that were in charge of different things. For example, members of the Centuriate Assembly took care of everyday business. Much later in Roman history, the Plebeian Assembly was formed to look after the interests of the poor, who were called **plebians**.

WORDS to KNOW

king: male ruler of land and people.

republic: a kind of government system with elected officials.

emperor: the ruler of an empire.

empire: the period of time in Roman history when emperors ruled.

Senate: a group of men who worked together to govern ancient Rome.

consul: a government official in charge of the military.

plebeian: the lowest-ranking Roman citizen. They were the lower class.

citizen: a member of a city or country who enjoys certain rights.

tribune: an elected official who looked out for the rights of plebeians.

MILITARY LEADERS TOOK OVER DIFFERENT COUNTRIES AND THEY WERE HAPPY...

UNTIL THEY DECIDED THEY WANTED EACHOTHER'S LAND... THEY FOUGHT PRETTY BADLY.

Members of the Plebeian Assembly elected officials called **tribunes** to represent them. Over the years, officials were elected to do other things, such as count how many people there were and keep track of money.

The Senate worked in buildings at the Forum, the city square in the center of Rome.

The End of the Republic

Rome was a republic for almost five hundred years. But many military generals got into politics and this caused problems. The military leaders wanted more power for themselves. After they fought and took over an area, they declared themselves the leaders. Pretty soon, there were many generals ruling lots of different areas. These military leaders declared themselves dictators. A dictator is someone who has all the power because he took it. Then, these dictators fought each other for control of more and more land. One of the more famous Roman dictators was Julius Caesar.

then & now

then: only senators got to vote for government leaders.

now: all citizens of Italy get to vote for government leaders.

In 46 BCE, Caesar made himself "dictator for life" over Rome. Although he ruled for only two years, Caesar accomplished a lot. He started many building projects, which included improving the Senate building. He also made social changes. For example, he created Roman colonies and gave lots of people citizenship. One of the things he is best remembered for is the change he made to the Roman calendar. Instead of a 355-day year, he made it a 365-day year. This "Julian" calendar is the one we use today.

Even though he was a good leader, the Senate didn't like Caesar. They thought he was too popular and too powerful. A group of over 60 senators plotted to kill Caesar. In March of 44 BCE, some of them stabbed him to death. Over a thousand years later, the great writer William Shakespeare wrote a play about Caesar's murder.

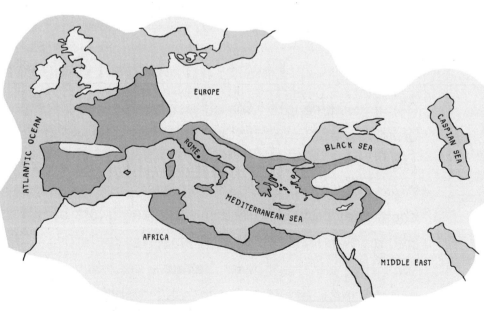

■ ROMAN LANDS DURING THE MID-REPUBLIC

The Age of Augustus

Since he had no son, Caesar adopted his great-nephew Octavian. Caesar did this so he could pass power on to someone in his family. After Caesar's death, Octavian fought with a man named Marc Antony for control of the empire (Marc Antony was married to Octavian's sister). Antony was also in love with Cleopatra, the Queen of Egypt. Julius Caesar had been in love with Cleopatra too. It was like some mixed-up soap opera! Octavian won control, and in 27 BCE the Senate made him the first emperor and renamed him Augustus. An emperor is a ruler of an empire. Sometimes emperors were elected and sometimes a family member handed the title down.

Augustus called himself princeps, which meant "first citizen." The people of Rome liked Augustus. He acted like one of them by eating simple foods and sleeping in a simple bed. Augustus was a good emperor. He expanded the Roman Empire by conquering other territory. He built many new roads. These roads opened up trade with other regions and helped Rome become even more successful. Augustus also had many crumbling temples fixed. He built new buildings, such as theaters.

Augustus brought much-needed peace to Rome. His rule is known as the Age of Augustus. When Augustus died, in 14 CE, the Senate declared him a god.

WOW

The month of July was named after Julius Caesar. Pretty cool, uh?

More Emperors

After Augustus, emperors ruled ancient Rome for the next 400 years. Some of them were good and kind leaders. Others were terrible and very mean. Two examples of terrible leaders were Caligula and Nero.

Caligula was the son of a war hero, and Rome had high hopes for him. Not long after becoming emperor, Caligula became very ill. He recovered, but began acting very strangely. He began telling everyone he was a god. He declared that his horse should be a senator! Worse, he began killing his friends, enemies, and strangers on the street. Eventually, some of Caligula's advisors killed him.

WOW

Can you guess which month is named after Augustus? Yep! August.

Emperor Nero wasn't much better. He killed members of his family, and even tried to kill his own mother! To top it off, Nero reportedly set a fire that burned two-thirds of Rome. The fire lasted a week. Some people claimed to have seen Nero singing and dancing as the fire raged. After he was declared a public enemy, Nero killed himself.

One of the good Roman emperors was Trajan. Trajan was very popular with the people of Rome. He was handsome, confident, and an excellent military leader. He got along well with the Senate. Under his rule, many lands were added to the Roman Empire.

He helped poor children by creating a government program that provided food. He also built many beautiful structures, such as Trajan's Forum and Trajan's Market.

Another good and popular emperor was Hadrian. Hadrian is famous for two things. The first is the Pantheon, a beautiful temple. The second is the wall he built. Hadrian's Wall was a long, stone wall between England and Scotland. It was supposed to keep invaders out and Romans in. It was about 80 miles long, 15 feet high, and 10 feet wide. Soldiers were stationed all along the wall, and ditches were dug on both sides of it. Hadrian's Wall was an amazing structure. Today, much of the wall is still standing and visitors can see and walk beside it.

PROPERTY OF HADRIAN

The Roman Army

Good emperors were only part of the reason the Roman Empire was so powerful. The main reason was its army.

The Roman army was made up mainly of **legionnaires** and **auxiliaries**. Legionnaires were Roman foot soldiers who signed up to be in the army for 20 to 25 years. Rome had 28 groups of soldiers. These groups were called legions. Each legion had around 5,000 or 6,000 soldiers. These men were well equipped. They had shields, armor, and weapons such as daggers, swords, and javelins. Auxiliaries were soldiers who came from Roman **provinces** but who were not Roman citizens. Provinces were lands that had been conquered by Roman armies that became part of the Roman Empire.

JUST FOR LAUGHS

Q: Why did the Roman soldier cross the road?

A: To conquer the other side!

Spartacus

Spartacus was a soldier from Greece. In 73 BCE, he was captured and sold as a slave to fight as a gladiator. While he was training at gladiator school, he started a riot and escaped. He took 70 other slaves with him. They hid on Mount Vesuvius. Other runaway slaves and criminals joined them. The group grew, and eventually Spartacus had an army of 90,000 men! Spartacus and his men fought the Roman army and even beat two legions. Since Spartacus had been trained as an auxiliary in Greece, he knew how to fight the Roman soldiers. He led the biggest slave revolt the Roman Empire had ever experienced. After two years of fighting and standing up for himself and other slaves, Spartacus was caught and put to death.

Cool Artifact

An *aquilifer* was the person who led a military legion into battle. To make sure all the soldiers could see him, the aquilifer carried a long pole with a golden eagle on top. This pole was called the standard.

The Roman army also had smaller groups of soldiers called centuries. Each **century** had around 100 men and was led by a soldier called a centurion. Besides legionnaires, auxiliaries, and centuries, the army had cavalry soldiers. These soldiers rode horses.

Life in the Roman army was tough. When they weren't fighting, soldiers had to train and march. They had to carry their own supplies on marches and in battle. Supplies included weapons, a sleeping roll, tools, water, pots and pans, dishes, and rations. Rations are the food a soldier carries for himself. Soldiers carried their things by attaching them to a cross-shaped stick. A soldier's pack could weigh over 50 pounds! Besides protecting the Empire's borders and conquering neighboring lands, soldiers were in charge of building. They built roads and bridges and forts.

Roman soldiers were famous for being good at fighting and defending themselves in battle. One really neat way they defended themselves from attack was the Roman "tortoise." Soldiers would stand very close together in a rectangle. The men on the outsides of the group would hold their shields off to the sides. The men in the middle would hold their shields over their heads. This formation made the group look like a turtle hiding in its shell! It also kept the enemies' arrows and javelins from hurting them. Wasn't that clever?

Citizenship

Romans were divided into three groups: citizens, non-citizens, and slaves. Citizens were men who were born in the Roman Empire. They were divided into three other groups. The **patricians** were very wealthy and were from the oldest Roman families. The **equites** were the middle-class businessmen. The plebeians were the ordinary, lower-class people. Being a Roman citizen was a good thing. It meant you had rights. For example, you could vote. Women were not considered citizens.

In addition to women, non-citizens were men who lived in Rome, but weren't born there. People who lived in the provinces weren't citizens either. Sometimes, foreigners could become citizens. The Senate did this to reward someone. You could become a citizen if you gave the Senate a lot of money! Slaves were not citizens. They had no rights. Freed slaves could become citizens, though.

WORDS to KNOW

legionnaires: professional soldiers in ancient Rome who were Roman citizens.

auxiliaries: professional soldiers in ancient Rome who were from the provinces and were not Roman citizens.

provinces: areas that were conquered and controlled by the Roman empire.

century: a unit of 100 men in the ancient Roman army.

patricians: the highest ranking Roman citizens. They were from the wealthiest families.

equites: Roman citizens who were middle class. For example, a business owner or solider.

Play "When in Rome"

There is a saying, "When in Rome, do as the Romans do." This game is based on that advice.

First, choose someone to be emperor. The emperor stands in front of the group, where all the players can see him or her. When the emperor is ready, he or she starts performing an action. For example, hopping on one foot, patting his or her head, or making a silly face. Everyone in the group has to pay close attention to the emperor and imitate his or her action. To make the game challenging, the emperor should change actions quickly and often.

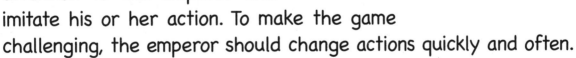

The emperor looks around and tries to catch someone not paying attention. The last player to copy the emperor's action must sit down. Keep playing until only one player is left standing. That last player becomes the new emperor and the old emperor joins the other players.

Make a Roman Coin

Coins were introduced to ancient Rome around 270 BCE. Before then, Romans traded goods for other goods. Roman coins were made of gold, silver, or bronze and often had the face of the emperor on one side. You'll need a grown-up to help with this project.

1 Spread the newspaper over your work area. Use the fabric paint to decorate one side of a wooden disc. You can make your profile or the profile of a real or imaginary emperor. A profile is the side view of someone's face. Let the paint dry completely.

2 Turn the disc over and decorate the other side. Roman coins often had symbols of strength or power on the backs of them. For example, they showed ships or soldiers. Let the paint on this side dry before moving on.

3 Follow the directions on the can to spray-paint one side of the coin. When the paint is dry to the touch, turn the coin over and paint the other side. Let the paint dry completely before touching the coin again. When the paint is dry, you'll have a Roman-style coin. Make more coins using any leftover discs and paint!

Variation: instead of wooden discs, you can cut circles out of cardboard. Just make sure the cardboard is thick. Otherwise, it will curl up when you spray-paint it.

Supplies

newspaper
small (coin size)
wooden discs*
fabric paint
gold, silver, or bronze
spray-paint

* Available at any craft store.

78

Write Your Own Rules

Ancient Roman laws were posted on bronze plaques in the Forum. Some of these laws might seem strange to us. For example, you were allowed to kill a robber if he broke into your house at night, but not if he broke into your house during the day. These plaques were called the Twelve Tables.

If you were in charge, what rules would you have? Make up your own rules, write them down on a piece of paper or poster board, and then hang them up. See if you can think of 12.

Get creative! For instance, maybe you can make a rule saying everyone must chew gum on Mondays. Number your rules with Roman numerals: I, II, III, IV, V, VI, VII, VIII, IX, X, XI, XII.

Supplies

piece of white paper or poster board
colorful markers

Gods and Goddesses

The Roman people worshiped many **gods** and **goddesses**. They believed these gods and goddesses took care of them. They also believed the gods and goddesses could cause bad things to happen if they were unhappy.

Most of the Roman gods and goddesses were similar to the ones from Greece. Gods were also borrowed from Egypt. For example, the Egyptian goddess Isis was worshiped throughout the Roman Empire. Roman gods looked human and each had a different job. For example, Mercury was in charge of bringing messages from the gods. The god Mithras protected soldiers.

Two of the most important gods were Jupiter and Juno. Jupiter was king of gods. His job was to protect the Roman lands. Juno was his wife. Her job was to protect women and marriages. Here are a few more important gods and goddesses and their jobs. I bet you recognize some of their names!

Diana: **goddess of the moon and hunting**
Mars: god of war
Venus: goddess of love
Neptune: god of the sea
Apollo: god of the sun and the arts
Pluto: god of the underworld

Each god had his or her own **temple**. A temple was a god's home on Earth. Many temples were made of stone and had large columns. People didn't worship gods at temples. But they did leave gifts, called offerings, at altars in front of the temples. Altars are small tables in special places, such as churches or temples. Offerings were to honor the gods and make them happy. They were also to thank the gods for help.

Shrines

Each ancient Roman home had a shrine. Shrines were shelves or spaces carved in walls where statues of gods were kept. They were kind of like mini temples. Families prayed every night and left offerings, such as bits of food, to gods. Household gods were special gods that ancient Romans believed looked out for families at home. A god called Janus protected the home's entrance. Lares were spirits of a family's ancestors, and they protected the house and fields. Other spirits called Penates protected the family's food.

Priests

Ancient Rome had **priests**. Priests were in charge of religious life. The emperor was the head priest. It was his job to act as a messenger between the gods and the Roman people. The emperor was called the pontifex maximus, which meant chief bridge-builder. The emperor was supposed to be the bridge between heaven and Earth.

Today, we think of priests as people who lead worship. Ancient Roman priests didn't lead people in worship, though. It was their job to take care of the temples. Others, called victimariuses, were in charge of making sacrifices. This meant killing an animal to offer to a god.

There were other religious leaders as well. They also had special jobs. Augers helped predict the future and advise emperors and the Senate on when it was a good time to do something, such as pass a law.

Vestal Virgins

Rome had female priests, called priestesses. These priestesses are better known as the **Vestal Virgins**. Vestal Virgins were in charge of taking care of the Temple of Vesta and keeping the temple fire burning. Vesta was the goddess of home. Girls between the ages of six and ten could become Vestal Virgins. They had to come from a free family and were picked through a lottery. A lottery is when a person's name is chosen from a collection of names. Once they were chosen, girls had to serve for 30 years! Vestal Virgins were not allowed to marry or have boyfriends. If they did, they could be put to death.

The Pantheon: a Famous Temple

One of the most famous buildings of ancient Rome is the Pantheon. You can still visit this ancient temple today, but it's not the original building! In 27 CE, Emperor Augustus's friend Marcus Agrippa designed the first Pantheon. It was built as a temple to honor the gods. The word pantheon is Greek for "all of the gods." The original Pantheon burned down in 80 CE.

Between 118 and 125 CE, Emperor Hadrian had a new, bigger Pantheon built. This building still stands today. The Pantheon is famous for its beautiful and amazing dome ceiling. The dome ceiling, made of concrete, is 142 feet in diameter. From the top of the dome to the floor is also 142 feet. This makes the dome look like a ball that's been cut exactly in half!

At the top of the dome there is a circular opening, called an ocular, that is 27 feet around. This hole lets in light. It also helps distribute weight so the ceiling doesn't collapse. To help hold up the heavy dome, the builders made the walls 20 feet thick! The floors of the Pantheon are made of marble. And, outside of the entrance of the building, there are 16 marble columns.

To predict the future, an auger studied birds. Romans believed birds could help bring messages from the gods. Haruspices were people who studied the remains of a sacrificed animal. It was their job to tell if the gods had accepted the sacrifice.

Christianity

Christianity is a religion that started during ancient Roman times. Instead of believing in lots of gods, Christians believed in one god. This went against just about everything most Romans believed, and it was a problem at first. Romans did not accept early Christians. In fact, Christianity was outlawed. Some Romans thought that being Christian meant you were against Rome. Romans were very mean to Christians. They forced them into slavery. Christians were even thrown to the lions in the Colosseum! Early Christians had to hide in underground passages called the catacombs to pray. These catacombs are still under the streets of Rome. Christians also used the catacombs as a cemetery.

JUST FOR LAUGHS

Q: What would be a good nick name for the Pantheon?

A: The Rome Dome!

Even though Christians were treated cruelly, Christianity spread throughout Rome. People probably liked the idea of having one god. Also, Christianity accepted everyone. It didn't care if you were rich or poor, free or a slave. In 313 CE, Emperor Constantine became a Christian. He made Christianity the state religion and built the first Christian churches. He also put an end to gladiator fighting.

WOW

Today, the Roman Catholic Church is one of the largest Christian religions. The head of the church, the pope, lives in Vatican City. Vatican City is an independent nation within the city of Rome. It is the smallest country in the world.

The End of the Roman Empire

During the time Christianity was spreading, the Roman Empire was losing its power. Enemies were attacking along the edges of the empire. Part of the problem was that the empire was too big for one person to rule. It was also too big to defend. Bit by bit, the Roman Empire lost its land and got smaller.

The Roman Empire had been split into two parts before Emperor Constantine came along: an eastern empire and a western empire. Each half of the empire had two emperors, because the job was too big for just one emperor.

The problem with having four emperors was that they began to fight with one another. Constantine was one of them. Emperors can have a hard time sharing, especially when it comes to deciding who is in charge.

In 312 CE, right about when he became a Christian, Emperor Constantine took over both halves of the empire. Constantine thought the city of Rome represented the past. Rome was in the western part. He wanted something new and exciting. Right away, he looked for a new capital city in the Eastern Empire. He chose a place called Byzantium. He named this new capital city **Constantinople**, after himself. Constantinople is still around, but it has a new name. It's called Istanbul, and it is a city in Turkey.

Unfortunately, the Roman Empire didn't stay united for long. Enemies kept attacking. In 410 CE, German soldiers took over the city of Rome. Soon after, the Western Empire disappeared altogether.

What happened to the eastern Roman empire? That's a good question. Because it was so far away from the city of Rome, it was safer from invaders. In fact, the Eastern Empire lasted for another thousand years! There were still many changes. Since Constantinople was closer to Greece than Rome, the Greeks became more important. For example, the Romans stopped speaking Latin and started speaking Greek.

Today, we call this empire the Byzantine Empire. This is because Constantinople was originally named Byzantium.

WORDS to KNOW

god: a being that is believed to have special powers and is worshiped.

goddess: a female god.

temple: beautiful buildings where the Roman gods "lived."

Pantheon: an ancient Roman temple famous for its dome ceiling.

priests: religious leaders who took care of the Roman temples.

Vestal Virgins: Roman priestesses who were in charge of keeping the temple fire at the Temple of Vesta burning.

Constantinople: the new capital of the Roman Empire built by Emperor Constantine.

Make a Votive

A votive was a small gift the Romans gave to a god to help heal a body part. The Romans shaped votives like the real body part! You can make your votive in the shape of anything you want be good at or improve.

1 Unwrap the soap. Grate the entire bar onto the wax paper. Be careful not to get your fingers too close to the grater!

2 Dip your fingers into the water. Let them get good and wet. Pick up some of the soap flakes and squeeze them together.

3 Use your hands to add a little bit of water to the soap flakes. Keep adding water and squeezing the soap flakes until you can mold them. The soap should feel like soft, wet, modeling clay.

4 You can mold the soap into any votive shape you'd like. For example, you could make a leg, arm, hand, or ear. Or, make your votive into a soccer ball if you dream of being a good soccer player, or shape it into a dancer if you want to dance.

5 Let your votive dry and harden. This will take a couple of hours.

6 Since you probably don't live near a Roman temple, you can make your own altar on a shelf. Arrange special things with your votive—a lucky pebble, pretty flower, favorite souvenir. Make more votives for your altar. Or you can put your votive in a soap dish and use it for your next bath!

Supplies

bar of soap
coarse food grater
wax paper
small bowl of warm water

abacus: an early calculator using beads or counters on rods to add and subtract.

altar: a small table inside or in front of a temple where gifts were left for the gods or animal sacrifices were made.

amphitheater: an oval or circular building with rising tiers of seats around a central open space used in ancient Rome for spectacles and contests.

amphorae: pottery jars used to store wine and olive oil.

amulet: special charm that protects the wearer.

aqueduct: a channel that carried water from streams in the hills and mountains and from the Tiber River to ancient Rome.

arch: a design element that the Romans used to build aqueducts and other buildings.

arena: an area for the presentation of sports events and other entertainment.

auxiliaries: professional soldiers from the provinces who were not Roman citizens.

basilica: a public building used as a court-house or gathering hall in Rome.

bathhouse: a building with public, indoor pools where Romans met to relax and socialize.

BCE: the abbreviation for Before Common Era.

bulla: a locket-like necklace worn by children.

cameo: small carvings of a person's profile.

castellum: a water tank in ancient Rome.

CE: the abbreviation for Common Era.

century: a unit of 100 men in the ancient Roman army.

channel: a canal through which a stream of water moves.

chariot: a small vehicle with wheels and a platform, pulled by horses.

Circus Maximus: an ancient Roman chariot racetrack.

citizen: a member of a city or country with certain rights.

Cloaca Maxima: a famous sewer in Rome.

Colosseum: ancient Rome's biggest amphi-theater.

comedy: a funny play.

Constantine: a Roman emperor who ruled from 324 to 337 CE. For a time, he reunited the two halves of the Roman Empire. He also made Christianity the state religion.

Constantinople: the capital of the Roman Empire late in its history, built by Emperor Constantine.

consul: government official in charge of the military.

emperor: the ruler of an empire.

empire: a territory ruled by an emperor. The period of time in ancient Roman history when emperors ruled.

equite: a middle-class Roman citizen, such as a business owner or solider.

ferment: the process where something with a lot of energy, like grain, breaks down into a simpler substance, like beer.

fibula: a special pin used by both men and women to hold their clothes in place.

forum: an open area, or town square, where Romans shopped or met to do business.

fresco: wall painting made on wet plaster.

frieze: a narrow, horizontal, decorative panel.

gladiators: slaves who were forced to fight as sport.

god: a being that is believed to have special powers and is worshiped.

goddess: a female god.

grammar school: a school where Roman children learned Greek and Latin grammar.

Hadrian: a popular Roman emperor. He built a big wall and rebuilt the Pantheon.

hobnail boots: boots that Roman soldiers wore with short nails in the soles.

insulae: apartments in ancient Rome.

Julius Caesar: a famous Roman dictator.

keystone: the top stone in an arch.

king: the male ruler of a kingdom.

Knucklebones: a Roman game where players tossed small bones into the air and tried to catch them on the backs of their hands.

legionnaires: professional soldiers in ancient Rome who were Roman citizens.

mosaic: a picture or design made from tiny tiles or stones set in cement.

ofellae: an ancient Roman version of pizza. It was bread with onions, fish, and olives to top. Tomatoes and cheese came much later.

orators: public speakers.

palla: a woolen shawl worn by women in ancient Rome.

Pantheon: an ancient Roman temple famous for its dome.

pantomime: a story told through body movement or facial expressions, without any words.

paterfamilias: the male head of a Roman household.

patricians: the highest-ranking Roman citizens, from the wealthiest families.

plebeians: the lowest-ranking Roman citizens.

priests: religious leaders who took care of the temples.

primary school: a public school where Roman children learned reading and math.

provinces: areas that were conquered and controlled by the Roman Empire.

republic: a kind of government with elected officials.

rhetoric school: a school where Roman students learned to be good public speakers.

Roman Empire: all the different lands and people ruled by Rome.

rote: learning by memorization.

Senate: a group of men who governed ancient Rome.

senator: a government official in ancient Rome who was a member of the senate.

slave: a person who, in the eyes of the law, belongs to another person.

Spartacus: a gladiator who started a revolt.

stola: a long dress worn by ancient Roman women.

strigil: a long, metal tool ancient Romans used to scrape dirt off their bodies.

temple: beautiful buildings where the Roman gods "lived."

thermopolia: small carts or shops where ancient Romans could buy inexpensive prepared food.

tiers: rows arranged one above another.

toga: a long, dress-like wrap worn by men.

tragedy: a sad play.

Trajan: a popular Roman emperor.

Trajan's Column: a 100-foot-high column carved with scenes of Trajan's victory over the Dacians.

Trajan's Market: an indoor market built during the reign of the emperor Trajan.

tribunes: elected officials who looked out for plebeians.

triclinium: an ancient Roman dining room. It meant three couches or three-sided couch.

trident: a kind of pitchfork.

tunic: an ancient Roman garment that looked like a long, sleeveless T-shirt.

Books and Periodicals

Bramblett, Reid, and Jeffrey Kennedy. *Top 10 Rome*. London: Dorling Kindersley, 2002.

Chrisp, Peter. *Make It Work! The Roman Empire*. Chicago: World Book, Inc., and Two-Can Publishing, 1998.

Connolly, Peter, and Hazel Dodge. *The Ancient City: Life in Classical Athens and Rome*. Oxford: Oxford Press, 1998.

Dickinson, Rachel. *Tools of the Ancient Romans*. White River Junction, VT: Nomad Press, 2006.

James, Simon. *Eyewitness Ancient Rome*. New York: Dorling Kindersley, 2004.

Macdonald, Fiona. *100 Things You Should Know About Ancient Rome*. Great Bardfield, England: Miles Kelly Publishing, 2003.

Macdonald, Fiona. *I Wonder Why Romans Wore Togas and Other Questions About Ancient Rome*. New York: Kingfisher, 1997.

Nelson, Eric. *The Complete Idiot's Guide to the Roman Empire*. New York: Alpha, 2002.

Staccioli, R.A. *Rome Monuments: Past and Present*. Arcole, Italy: Vision S.R.L., 2001.

Steele, Philip. *History in Stone: Ancient Rome*. San Diego: Silver Dolphin, 2001.

Documentaries

Rome: Engineering an Empire. Discovery History Channel, 2007.

Seven Wonders of Ancient Rome. Films Media Group, 2004.

"Episode 3: Hannibal and the Colosseum." *Drive Through History: Rome*. Coldwater Media, 2005.

Web Sites

"The Romans"
http://www.bbc.co.uk/schools/romans/

"Secrets of Lost Empires"
http://www.pbs.org/wgbh/nova/lostempires/roman/

"Who Were the Romans?"
http://www.brims.co.uk/romans/

"The Roman Empire in the 1st Century"
http://www.pbs.org/empires/romans/empire/index.html

"Ancient Rome"
http://www.kidskonnect.com/AncientRome/
AncientRomeHome.html

Neat Web Sites to Check Out

Don't miss this site! It has plenty of awesome stuff to check out and fun quizzes.
http://www.bbc.co.uk/schools/romans/

This is the children's page from the Roman Empire site. It has some great pictures.
http://www.roman-empire.net/children/index.html

This site has lots of fun and interesting articles about life in Rome.
http://www.kidskonnect.com/AncientRome/
AncientRomeHome.html

This site has some neat photos.
http://www.historyforkids.org/learn/romans/

This site has lots of information and a great glossary.
http://www.socialstudiesforkids.com/subjects/ancientrome.htm

Fun Museums with Ancient Rome Collections

The Cleveland Museum of Art (Cleveland, OH)
The Metropolitan Museum of Art (New York, NY)
Los Angeles County Museum of Art (Los Angeles, CA)
Michael C. Carlos Museum (Atlanta, GA)
Museum of Fine Arts (Boston, MA)
Nelson-Atkins Museum of Art (Kansas City, MO)
University of Pennsylvania (Philadelphia, PA)
Worcester Art Museum (Worcester, MA)

More Cool Books to Read

Altman, Susan, and Susan Lechner. *Ancient Rome (Modern Rhymes about Ancient Times)*. Danbury, CT: Children's Press, 2002.

Ancient Rome (DK Revealed). New York: DK Publishing, 2003.

Carlson, Lauri. *Classical Kids: An Activity Guide to Life in Ancient Greece and Rome*. Chicago: Chicago Review Press, 1998.

If I Were a Kid in Ancient Rome. Peterborough, NH: Cobblestone Publishing, 2007.

Malam, John, and David Salariya. *You Wouldn't Want to be a Roman Gladiator!* London: Franklin Watts, 2001.

Osborne, Mary Pope, and Natalie Pope Boyce. *Ancient Rome and Pompeii (Magic Tree House Research Guides)*. New York: Random House Books for Young Readers, 2006.

Index

M
makeup, 59
maps, 67, 70
marble, 14, 20, 83
Mediterranean Sea, 2, 3
military and soldiers, 49, 63, 68, 69, 72–76, 78, 80
money, 25, 49, 50, 69, 76, 78
mosaics, 2, 14, 15, 19
Mount Vesuvius, 18, 74
music, 27, 40, 47

N
Nero, 72
numbers, 39–42, 49

O
orators and public speaking, 39, 40, 44, 45
oscilla, 20, 21

P
Pantheon, 73, 83, 84, 86
plebeians, 68, 69
Pompeii, 18
poor people, 5, 14–16, 25, 28, 38, 58, 63, 68, 73, 84
priests, 82, 83, 86

R
religion, 80–87
roads, 1, 5, 6, 10, 12, 71, 75
Roman numerals, 39, 41, 42, 79
Roman Empire, 1, 3, 4, 6, 29, 50, 57, 67–76, 80, 85, 86
Roman Republic, 67–69
Rome's founding, 2, 3

S
school and education, 38–42
Senate and senators, 58, 61, 68–73, 76, 82
sewer, 3, 5, 15
slaves, 14, 15, 17, 50–52, 59, 74, 76, 84
soldiers and military, 49, 63, 68, 69, 72–76, 78, 80
Spartacus, 74
statues, 14, 30, 81
stone, 4, 6, 7, 14, 30, 48, 50, 81
storytelling, 27

T
temples, 30, 71, 73, 81–83, 86, 87
theater, 47, 48, 54–56, 71
Tiber River, 2–4
togas, 58, 60, 61, 64, 65
toys and games, 40
Trajan, 2, 29, 30, 49, 72, 73
Trajan's Column, 29, 30, 36, 37, 73
Trajan's Market, 29, 30, 73
tribune, 68, 69

V
Vestal Virgins, 82, 86
volcanoes, 4, 18

W
water, 1–6, 9, 13–17
wealthy people, 5, 13, 14, 16, 26, 27, 38, 58, 59, 61, 68, 76, 84
weapons, 50–52, 74, 75
Western Empire, 85, 86